# missing mother, fondest friend

*poems by*

# Lia Patricia James

*Finishing Line Press*
Georgetown, Kentucky

# missing mother, fondest friend

Copyright © 2021 by Lia Patricia James
ISBN 978-1-64662-697-7 First Edition
All rights reserved under International and Pan-American Copyright Conventions. No part of this book may be reproduced in any manner whatsoever without written permission from the publisher, except in the case of brief quotations embodied in critical articles and reviews.

## ACKNOWLEDGMENTS

Endless thanks are due to my professor, Heather Corbally Bryant, for your enthusiastic encouragement and your constant reminders that I need no one's permission to claim and pursue my dreams.

Thanks, also, are due to all the special friends who graciously lent bits of your souls to the following verses.

To Savana, my incredible sister, for bravely experiencing your grief in tandem with mine. And to Dad, for continuing to get up and show up every day. Thank you.

Finally, I dedicate these words to my beloved mother, Pascale, and to my dear friend, Emma.

Thank you, Emma, for the absolute most magical childhood anyone could've wished for. Thank you, Mom. For everything. I miss you every day.

Special thanks to @nil.g_ on Instagram for the mother-daughter silhouette on the cover.

Publisher: Leah Huete de Maines
Editor: Christen Kincaid
Cover Art and Design: Emma Jahki Wynter
Author Photo: Savana Michèle James

Order online: www.finishinglinepress.com
also available on amazon.com

Author inquiries and mail orders:
Finishing Line Press
PO Box 1626
Georgetown, Kentucky 40324
USA

# Table of Contents

mango memories ............................................................................. 1

I remember you ............................................................................. 2

haikus on day 2 ............................................................................. 3

haikus on real life imaginary friends ............................................ 4

invocation ...................................................................................... 5

let's cook ........................................................................................ 6

close to home ................................................................................ 8

hey, best friend ............................................................................ 10

halftime? ...................................................................................... 11

twice washed ............................................................................... 12

ashes to ashes .............................................................................. 13

where has my friend gone? ........................................................ 16

anatomy ....................................................................................... 17

Washing our hair ........................................................................ 20

**mango memories**

Sticky mango hands licked clean by sweet mango mouths.

Green mango smiles ripen with recognition.

Rotten mango words sour an argument, soon forgotten.

Clean mango seed hands, always happy to hold each other again.

**I remember you**

I used to remember you in vivid color.
Bright, tangible, living clips of memory.
Your embrace. Your laugh.
Your love.

But memory fades.

I remember you now in one monochrome moment.
Sat together reading in the library.
The curl of your hair.
Your smile.
Still, your love.

**haikus on day 2**

Your eggshell mattress
ended up being comfy—
it felt just like you.


Green juice in the fridge.
You would have drunk it today
if you were still here.


Your bedside's the same.
I won't let them clear it off.
But maybe they should.

**haikus on real life imaginary friends**

I like your pictures.
Where are you and where am I?
Can you paint me in?

Don't leave me again.
It's so hard to say goodbye.
Wait, just one more hug.

Won't you come back here?
I still want to play with you.
All alone again.

**invocation**

Write me a letter and never mail it.
Keep a box of your thoughts at my place.

Sing me another guava jelly gospel
at a Sunday Dinner that lasts all day.

Put me to sleep with one more kitchen sink lullaby
and wake me with a home-cooked lunch box morning prayer.

I wish my off-to-school memories of waving goodbye
were a bit more bleary-eyed.

For I would sacrifice any wide-awake wave for one more night
where your love song to an audience of after-dinner dishes
could have been a duet.

Why is it that the best time for dishes
seems to be halfway through the longest nights
even on the days when dinner ends at sunset?

Alone, I try conjuring you in a cup of tea.
I grasp at ginger-flavored memory.

>   I change into your t-shirt at 2am
>   and come alive,
>   hoping against all hope
>   that you will, too.

**let's cook**

let's cook like Mom did.

I never wrote down recipes
      or paid much attention to the
ingredients
         but I remember
         all the rules I'll never need like

how to keep the chicken breast moist and
how much cream cheese to use in the dip.

      so, let's try anyway.

and we'll fight over
how much salt and
parsley and
tomato and
garlic.

and we'll put
way too much black pepper
in the cheese sauce.

and we'll argue about tape on
christmas eve
and we'll hug in the kitchen.

and you'll preheat the oven
and put the pot on the fire.

and I'll try to act like I know better
and you'll sometimes let me.

hug me and whisper about how it all feels
and let me convince you
for once
that you're not alone.

then I'll apologize for everything and mourn those
    unfixable sadnesses
that we are living
    alone, together.

let's make the pasta
and be best friends
and love each other.

**close to home**

Getting home is
putting on a new skin
zipping it up quickly so that
no one knows
it's me.

I leave
myself
at the arrival gate
of the airport.

I abandon my flannels for frills
I hand in my converse and slide into sandals.

I don
sunglasses
handbag
nail polish
flowery dress.

I strip away
leg hair
armpits
sports bras
boots.

Give me a grocery list
laundry to fold
hair to control
a family to hold
together.

I am Momma, personified.
My mother incarnate.
Do they know who I am when I am not her?
Do I?
I slip into my skin at the end of each semester.
I am my mother.
I am home.
I am free.
I am
me.

**hey, best friend**

I've been trying to figure out how to say best friend in the almost past tense.

*best friend*

    i. the taste of [*pink*] milk that was always better in the bottles at your house.
    ii. the races up the stairs that I never won.
    iii. the trips across the sea just to see you.
    iv. all the times I you we got in trouble.
    v. the birthday parties where other people's speeches claimed my title.
    vi. the waves across the pews.
    vii. the song. *that* song.
    viii. the place that ~~was is~~ was ours.
    ix. the confessions we can't repeat.
    x. the nights we pretend not to remember.
    xi. the matching tattoos we (almost) got.
    xii. the years we didn't talk because
        I was too sad and it made you
            so sad you just couldn't
                bear it
      and then when you got
        too sad, too
           you couldn't
              bare yourself
      enough for me to give you
      the love neither of us knew
      was still there.
    xiii. *time.* nothing really goes wrong but somehow
      "*memories*"
    becomes a dormant word—
no longer something we make
but something we have.

## halftime?

It hasn't been six months, has it?
No, it's been twenty. Twenty today.
Where would you be right now
if you were?

If you were, and we were,
and our team wasn't missing a player.

If our season hadn't ended
and our hearts didn't need to be mended
and I didn't get offended
every time someone makes a *your mom* joke.

Yeah, they still make those.

**twice washed**

The laundry we used to fold together is now twice washed, my salt-stained cheeks aching for your inimitable comfort.

**ashes to ashes**


"Ashes, ashes we all fall down!"
    and she tickles me
    and a laugh like a penny in a fountain
    bubbles out of me.

Someone once told me that
that nursery rhyme was about the bubonic plague.
I don't really know if that's true.

Supposedly a pocket full of posies was supposed to
mask the smell of death.
I looked it up because
I wanted to start this poem differently
and now I don't really even know if this is a poem
anymore.

—

Ashes are a funny thing, aren't they?
We scatter them
and we put them into marbles
and the pious among us use them to make crosses on foreheads
once a year.

—

I look at her ashes sometimes
and wonder where in the world
she would want me to spread them
or what part of her is in those ashes
or whether a piece of her soul had stayed behind
in the ashes, too
just to smile back at me
when I kiss the jar first thing after getting home.

And I don't really want to know the science behind it,
so, no one tell me that really, it's all just bones.

Because as much as a stranger in an online forum wants me to think
that 'ring around the rosie' is about the black plague
and that the pocket full of posies is supposed to
cover the ugly smell of death

I will never be
*un*convinced
that within her ashes live:

the locks of her rapunzel hair
that grew faster than a child
in the summer after the 4th grade

and the secrets I whispered
that she kept without me asking

and the secrets I never told her
that she knew anyway

and the advice I will need
when I fall in love
        again
and out of it
and then back in love
and then get married
                      maybe

and all the things I don't know about
    changing a diaper
    and fighting with my kid
    and and
    and and and
    and

and the dreams of things only done
by people who live past forty-eight

and that laugh
and the way she wiped my tears
and the way she said those
        *things*
                she said


    and a piece of me, too.

**where has my friend gone?**

My time machine has a grass floor
and invisible walls
and a cloudy blue ceiling that I can't
touch.

I go on the walks we used to take
together
but going through the motions becomes
tricky
when you're not there to remind me.

I catch myself smiling
and the unfamiliar mask reminds me
of you.

**anatomy**

*What happens in your stomach when you mess up*

The hot acid of guilt bubbles up
into the pit of your stomach
and makes it
dance.

It twists and turns in a waltz and
steps on toes and
loses count and
tumbles.

*What happens in your chest when you realize you've fallen out of love*

That tight feeling
is actually
the rope you'd been
weaving
the whole time.

Except all of a sudden
there are all these knots and
the more you try to unravel them
the tighter they get
until

ouch.

And the rope breaks.
And the love seeps out of the frayed ends.

*That ball in your throat that shows up when you're trying not to cry*

It's filled with all the things that went wrong
surrounded by all the reasons not to break
and dammed by a wall of frail fear that
is slowly chipped away as
the ball does its best to squeeze its way out.

*What happens at the back of your neck when someone you love hurts you*

The hairs on your nape
become the spines of a cactus
and all of a sudden you're in the desert.

But you're cold.

And the hot desert sun hits your eyes and they
water
and water
and don't stop
until they've run out.


*Why your hands get clammy when you're holding your best friend's*

Your hands don't understand
that the sweat leaving them
isn't glue enough to
hold them together.

But they try
because what's the harm
in a couple of clammy hands
doing their best?

*What happens to a mother's heart when she sees that best friends have found each other again*

It bursts at the seams
because, it seems
your love
after all these years
never stopped growing.

**Washing our hair**

I had an angel of a mother. She used to wash my hair.

We would put the slotted wooden stool in her shower, and I would take off my clothes and sit while she wet and pulled and shampooed and rinsed and conditioned and combed with the gentlest, most delicate hands. I haven't a clue what we talked about for the two or three hours that it took to wash and comb my hair.

I sometimes wonder if I dreamed my childhood, because I don't remember when it stopped.

I do remember coming home from college. I remember seeing that her sickness had made it impossible to raise her hand over her head. I remember the first time I helped wash her hair. I put the slotted wooden stool in her shower. I could not wet and pull and shampoo and rinse and condition and comb like she did. I did not inherit the gentleness of her hands. That gentleness, I thought, I wasn't meant to learn until I had a daughter's hair to comb. Until I had my own slotted stool. This wasn't supposed to happen, yet.

*"Your hair is so beautiful, Momma."*

*"It's the only beautiful thing I have left."*

She was wrong, of course. I told her as much.

This, I know, I did not dream. I have an angel of a mother. I think of her when I wash my hair.

**L**ia Patricia James graduated with a BA in Anthropology and Spanish from Wellesley College. Born in 1999 to a Haitian mother and a Jamaican father, she has called Kingston, Jamaica home for all her life. Her writing has appeared in *The Wellesley Review* and in *Counterpoint: The Wellesley College Journal of Campus Life*. Lia has served as Managing Editor at The Unplug Collective since July 2020. She is now based in Brighton, England where she is pursuing her MA in Anthropology of Development and Social Transformation at the University of Sussex. *Missing mother, fondest friend* is her first poetry chapbook. More of Lia's poetry can be found on her blog, *52 Things That Matter*.

www.ingramcontent.com/pod-product-compliance
Lightning Source LLC
LaVergne TN
LVHW041525070426
835507LV00013B/1830